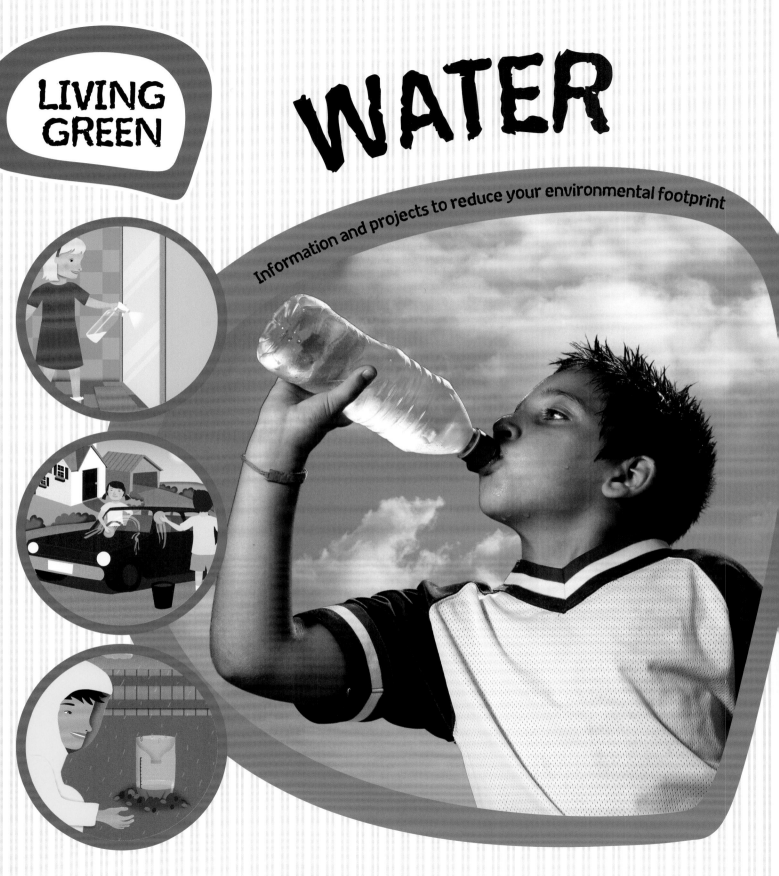

LIVING GREEN

WATER

Information and projects to reduce your environmental footprint

Marshall Cavendish
Benchmark
New York

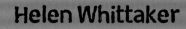
Helen Whittaker

This edition first published in 2012 in the United States of America by
Marshall Cavendish Benchmark
An imprint of Marshall Cavendish Corporation

Website: www.marshallcavendish.us

This publication represents the opinions and views of the author based on Helen Whittaker's personal experience, knowledge, and research. The information in this book serves as a general guide only. The author and publisher have used their best efforts in preparing this book and disclaim liability rising directly and indirectly from the use and application of this book.

Other Marshall Cavendish Offices:
Marshall Cavendish Ltd. 5th Floor, 32-38 Saffron Hill, London EC1N 8FH, UK • Marshall Cavendish International (Asia) Private Limited, 1 New Industrial Road, Singapore 536196 • Marshall Cavendish International (Thailand) Co Ltd. 253 Asoke, 12th Flr, Sukhumvit 21 Road, Klongtoey Nua, Wattana, Bangkok 10110, Thailand • Marshall Cavendish (Malaysia) Sdn Bhd, Times Subang, Lot 46, Subang Hi-Tech Industrial Park, Batu Tiga, 40000 Shah Alam, Selangor Darul Ehsan, Malaysia

Marshall Cavendish is a trademark of Times Publishing Limited

All websites were available and accurate when this book was sent to press.

Library of Congress Cataloging-in-Publication Data

Whittaker, Helen.
    Water / Helen Whittaker.
    p. cm. — (Living Green)
    Includes index.
    Summary: "Discusses how water use impacts the environment and what you
can do to be more eco-conscious"—Provided by publisher.
    ISBN 978-1-60870-576-4
    1. Water—Juvenile literature. 2. Environmentalism—Juvenile literature.
    I. Title.
    GB662.3.W485 2010
363.6' 1—dc22

                    2010044364

First published in 2011 by
MACMILLAN EDUCATION AUSTRALIA PTY LTD
15–19 Claremont Street, South Yarra 3141

Visit our website at www.macmillan.com.au or go directly to www.macmillanlibrary.com.au

Associated companies and representatives throughout the world.

Publisher: Carmel Heron
Commissioning Editor: Niki Horin
Managing Editor: Vanessa Lanaway
Editor: Georgina Garner
Proofreader: Helena Newton
Designer: Julie Thompson
Page layout: Julie Thompson, Raul Diche
Photo researcher: Claire Armstrong (management: Debbie Gallagher)
Illustrators: Nives Porcellato and Andrew Craig (**6, 10**); Cat MacInnes (all other illustrations)
Production Controller: Vanessa Johnson

Printed in China

Acknowledgments

The author and publisher are grateful to the following for permission to reproduce copyright material:

Front cover photograph: Boy drinking water bottle courtesy of iStockphoto.com/Erdosain. Front and back cover illustrations by Cat MacInnes.

Photographs courtesy of: Corbis, **8** (top), /JGI/Tom Grill, **28**, /Juice Images, **21**, /moodboard, **22**; iStockphoto.com/Andreyuu, **18**, /ansonsaw, **12** (steel), /APCortizasJr, **12** (paper), /bradwieland, **19** (right), /Greg da Silva, **31**, /hadynyah, **9** (top), /narvikk, **7** (bottom), /stevecoleccs, **3**, **24**; MEA Photos/Claire Armstrong, **26**; © Murray-Darling Basin Authority/Arthur Mostead, **11** (bottom); Photolibrary/Alamy/David Hoffman Photo Library, **13** (top), /Alamy/Picture Partners, **17**; Shutterstock/Akaiser, (environment icons, throughout), /alsamua, **6**, /Ashaki, **5** (top), /Katrina Brown, **4, 32**, /Jirka Bursik, **5** (bottom), /dcwcreations, **15**, /Elenaphotos21, **12** (petrol), /ejwhite, **7** (top), /FotoYakov, **10** (right), /Grisha, **10** (left), /gsmad, **30** (middle), /Péter Gudella, **12** (t-shirt), /Laenz, (eco icons, throughout), /mmaxer, **30** (top), /newphotoservice, **12** (plastic), /Denis & Yulia Pogostins, **14** (top), **19** (left), /puwanai, **13** (bottom), /riekephotos, **20**, /Moreno Soppelsa, **12** (top), /Eduard Stelmakh, **8** (bottom), /Jozsef Szsasz-Fabian, **14** (bottom), /Maksim Toome, **12** (car), /Peter Wollinga, **9** (bottom), /Ye, (recycle logos, throughout), /Jin Young Lee, **30** (bottom), /Arman Zhenikeyev, **11** (top).

While every care has been taken to trace and acknowledge copyright, the publisher tenders their apologies for any accidental infringement where copyright has proved untraceable. They would be pleased to come to a suitable arrangement with the rightful owner in each case.

Please note
At the time of printing, the Internet addresses appearing in this book were correct. Owing to the dynamic nature of the Internet, however, we cannot guarantee that all these addresses will remain correct.

Contents

Don't waste the rain—catch it!
page 24

Glossary Words

When a word is printed in **bold**, you can look up its meaning in the Glossary on page 31.

Turn saltwater into freshwater! Amazing! page 26

Living Green

Living green means choosing to care for the **environment** by living in a sustainable way.

Living Sustainably

Living sustainably means living in a way that protects Earth. Someone who lives sustainably avoids damaging the environment or wasting resources so that Earth can continue to provide a home for people in the future.

You and your friends can change your habits and behavior to help Earth. Living green makes sense!

How Our Actions Affect the Environment

Human activities use up Earth's **natural resources** and damage the environment. Some natural resources are **renewable**, such as wind and water, and some are **nonrenewable**, such as the **fossil fuels coal** and **oil**.

As the world's population grows, people are using more water, which creates water shortages, and are causing water **pollution**. We are using more nonrenewable resources too, which are usually mined from the earth and then burned, causing **habitat** destruction and air pollution. People cannot continue to live and act the way they do now—this way of life is unsustainable.

What Is an Environmental Footprint?

A person's environmental footprint describes how much damage that person does to the environment and how quickly the person uses up Earth's resources. A person who protects the environment and does not waste resources has a light environmental footprint. A person who pollutes the environment and wastes resources has a heavy environmental footprint.

Water

Understanding the environmental effects of water use can help us make greener choices and live more sustainably.

How Water Use Affects the Environment

Only 2.5 percent of all the water on Earth is freshwater. The remaining 97.5 percent is saltwater. The way we use freshwater affects the environment in two main ways: by causing water shortages and causing pollution.

The world's population is growing rapidly, and modern lifestyles use a lot of water. Unless we start to reduce our water use, one day soon there may not be enough water to go around.

Wastewater from homes, farms, and factories is released into the environment. This wastewater contains pollutants that harm plants and animals and can also affect human health.

Where to Next?

• To find out about the water cycle and how water use at home, in agriculture, and in industry affects the environment, go to the "Background Briefing" section on page 6.
• To try out fun projects that will help you reduce your environmental footprint, go to the "Living Green Projects" section on page 16.

How Does Taking a Hot Bath Affect the Environment?

Taking a hot bath has many effects on the environment. It can contribute to water shortages and water pollution.

Heating the Water

Most water is heated using natural gas or electricity, which uses up nonrenewable resources, pollutes the air, and contributes to **global warming**.

Filling the Bath

Filling a bath uses more water than taking a shower. Water is a limited resource, so using too much can cause water shortages.

Emptying the Bath

Wastewater from a bath contains **detergents** from soap, shower gel, or shampoo. Chemicals in these detergents can pollute the water cycle.

The Water Cycle

The water cycle is a natural process that allows us to use the same water again and again. It has been a sustainable cycle for millions of years, but people are now affecting this cycle.

How Earth's Water Cycle Works

1. The sun heats the oceans. Some of the water **evaporates** and becomes **water vapor**. The water vapor is lighter than the surrounding air, so it rises.

2. As the water vapor rises, it hits cold air and **condenses** to form water droplets. These clump together to make clouds. The water droplets in the clouds keep growing until they become too heavy for the air to hold them. They then fall back to Earth as **precipitation**, usually in the form of rain.

The water on Earth is continually moving around in a process called the water cycle.

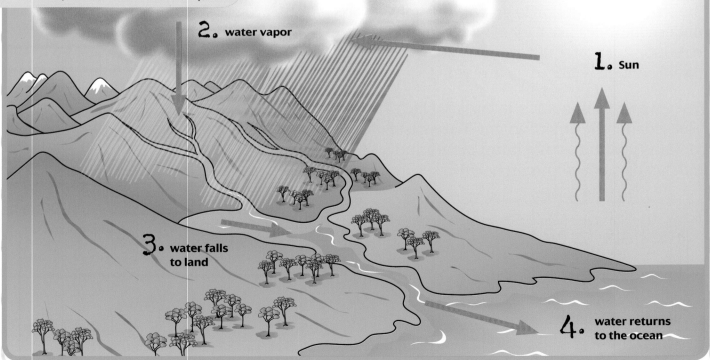

2. water vapor

1. Sun

3. water falls to land

4. water returns to the ocean

3. The water falls onto the land. Some of it soaks into the ground, some of it flows into streams and rivers, and some of it is used by plants, animals, and people.

4. Eventually, all the water finds its way back to the oceans. The water cycle begins again.

How We Affect the Water Cycle

People collect freshwater from rivers, lakes, and underground water sources and use it in their homes, farms, and businesses. Once water has been used, the sewage system carries away the dirty wastewater. In some parts of the world, wastewater is cleaned before it is returned to rivers, lakes, and oceans, but in other places it is not cleaned, so it pollutes the water cycle. In some areas, people are using freshwater at a faster rate than it can be cleaned and replaced by the natural water cycle.

How We Use Freshwater

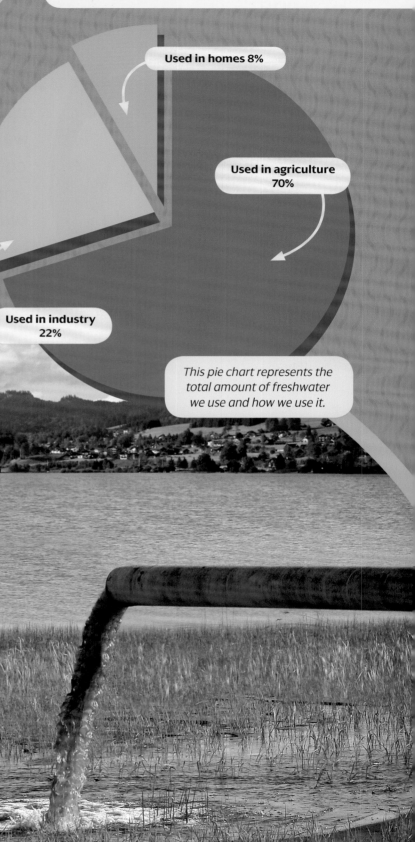

Used in homes 8%

Used in agriculture 70%

Used in industry 22%

This pie chart represents the total amount of freshwater we use and how we use it.

When waste water is released into the environment, it pollutes Earth's natural water cycle.

Water Use at Home

In wealthy countries, clean water is piped directly into homes. We use water in our homes for drinking and cooking, and to wash ourselves and clean our things. When we want water, we simply turn on a tap.

When you wash your car, you are taking freshwater from the tap and returning dirty water to the environment, as the water runs into the gutters and onto your lawn. Detergents in the water can pollute the environment.

How Water Is Used in the Home

We use water in many parts of the home, such as:
- in the kitchen, for drinking, cooking, and washing dishes
- in the bathroom, for washing hands, brushing teeth, and taking baths and showers
- in the laundry, for running the washing machine and washing things by hand
- in the toilet, for flushing the toilet
- outside, for watering the lawn and garden plants, growing fruit and vegetables, washing windows, and washing the car

How a Household Uses Freshwater Indoors

This pie chart shows how water is typically used in a home in a wealthy country, such as Australia, the United States, or Canada.

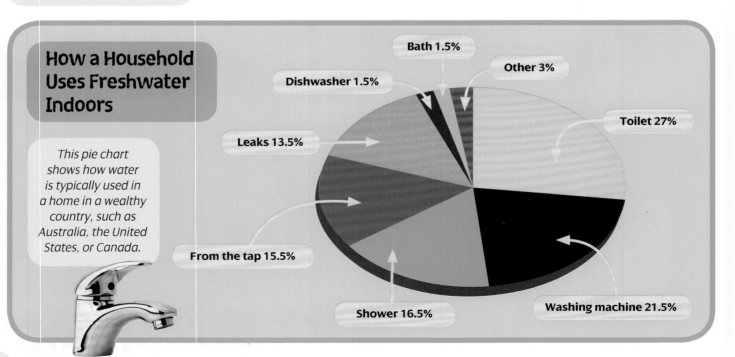

- Bath 1.5%
- Dishwasher 1.5%
- Other 3%
- Leaks 13.5%
- Toilet 27%
- From the tap 15.5%
- Shower 16.5%
- Washing machine 21.5%

The Environmental Impacts of Water Use at Home

Over the past hundred years, water use has been growing more than twice as fast as the world's population. In many parts of the world, water is in short supply. Using more water than necessary at home contributes to water shortages.

Household water use also contributes to water pollution. Wastewater from homes contains pollutants in the form of household chemicals such as detergents and **disinfectants**.

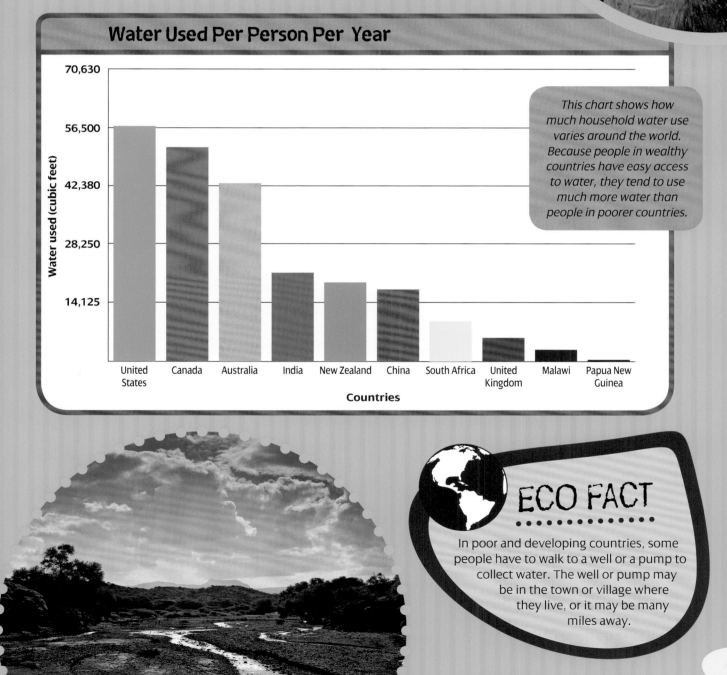

Water Used Per Person Per Year

Water used (cubic feet)

| 70,630 |
| 56,500 |
| 42,380 |
| 28,250 |
| 14,125 |

Countries: United States, Canada, Australia, India, New Zealand, China, South Africa, United Kingdom, Malawi, Papua New Guinea

This chart shows how much household water use varies around the world. Because people in wealthy countries have easy access to water, they tend to use much more water than people in poorer countries.

ECO FACT

In poor and developing countries, some people have to walk to a well or a pump to collect water. The well or pump may be in the town or village where they live, or it may be many miles away.

Water Use in Agriculture

Agriculture is the production of food through farming. Farms use thousands of gallons of water to grow the foods that eventually end up on our plates.

How Water Is Used in Agriculture

Water is needed to grow crops such as fruit, vegetables, and grains. In some places, rainfall provides crops with enough water, but in drier areas farmers have to provide water for their crops. They do this by taking freshwater from other areas, often using channels to move the water. This is called **irrigation**.

It takes more water to produce meat than to produce other types of food. Animals raised for their meat need to be given water to drink, and the grain that they are fed needs a lot of water to grow, too.

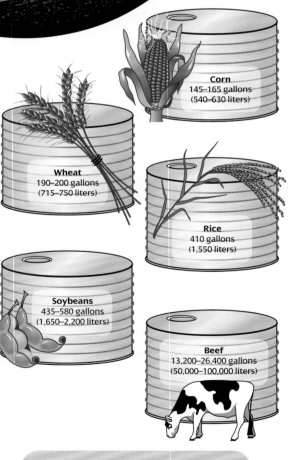

Corn
145–165 gallons
(540–630 liters)

Wheat
190–200 gallons
(715–750 liters)

Rice
410 gallons
(1,550 liters)

Soybeans
435–580 gallons
(1,650–2,200 liters)

Beef
13,200–26,400 gallons
(50,000–100,000 liters)

This illustration shows the amount of water needed to produce 2 pounds (1 kilogram) of various foods.

ECO FACT

It takes between 500 and 1,300 gallons (2,000–5,000 liters) of water to produce enough food for one person for one day.

The Environmental Impacts of Water Use in Agriculture

Agriculture uses huge amounts of water. When irrigation water is added to soil, it draws up salt that is stored below the surface. Over time, this can make the soil too salty to grow anything in, and the land becomes a desert.

Most farmers use artificial **fertilizers** to increase the amount that their crops produce and **pesticides** to control pests and diseases. These chemicals can get washed into streams and rivers, polluting them. Farmers who keep livestock have to get rid of effluent, which is manure and urine from the animals. This is another source of water pollution.

Salt in the soil, caused by irrigation, has caused this farming area of Victoria, Australia, to become a desert. This is one environmental impact of water use in agriculture.

Water Use in Industry

Industry makes all the products we buy. Almost every **manufactured** product uses water in one way or another at some stage of the manufacturing process.

How Water Is Used in Industry

Industry uses water in a variety of ways, depending on the product being manufactured. Some products contain water as an ingredient. Water may be used in the manufacture of other products, for washing or cooling, or for dissolving or diluting materials. Products that are manufactured using very large amounts of water are paper, oil, chemicals, and metals.

How Much Water Does It Take to Make?

Product	Gallons of water (liters)
2 pound (1 kg) steel	25 (95 liters)
2 pound (1 kg) plastic	55 (200 liters)
2 pound (1 kg) paper	85 (325 liters)
0.2 gallon (1 L) gasoline	2.5 (10 liters)
1 T-shirt	440 (1,650 liters)
1 car	40,000 (150,000 liters)

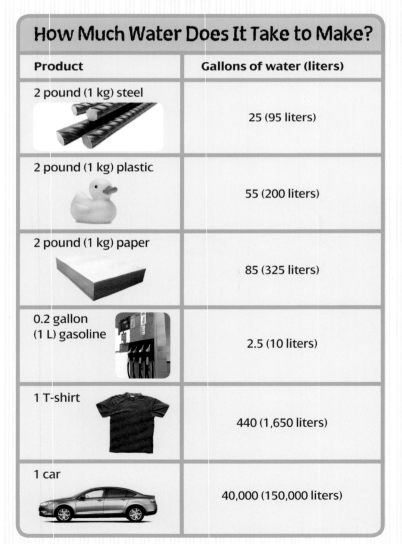

Industrial Water Use, 1995–2025

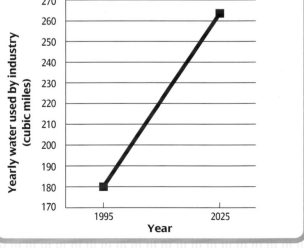

Between 1995 and 2025, the annual amount of water used by industry is expected to almost double.

The Environmental Impacts of Water Use in Industry

Almost all the water used by industry is freshwater, not saltwater. This puts pressure on water supplies used for drinking and growing food. Industry creates water pollution by releasing **contaminated** wastewater. Another type of industrial pollution is thermal pollution, which occurs when water that has been used for cooling is returned to the environment while it is still warm. Both of these types of pollution are harmful to animals and plants that live in water.

A factory releases water contaminated with grease and fat into a river. This pollution will affect the freshwater and the animals and plants that live in it.

ECO FACT

Worldwide, industry dumps between 300 and 500 million tons of pollutants into the water supply every year.

What Can You Do?

By making a few simple changes to your lifestyle, you can use less water and create less pollution. Knowing how much water is used to manufacture goods can help you make greener choices when you shop.

You can use gray water to water your garden. Collect gray water by keeping a watering can or a bucket in the shower.

Green Tips for Using Less Water at Home

You can use less water at home by:

 taking short showers instead of baths

 waiting until the washing machine is full before doing a load of laundry

 washing the family car using a bucket of water instead of a hose

✔ turning off the tap while you brush your teeth

 getting leaking taps fixed quickly

✔ collecting gray water at home. Gray water is wastewater that is clean enough to be used again for some things, such as water from the shower, bath, sinks, and washing machine. Using gray water means that you don't have to use more freshwater from the tap. You can use gray water to water the garden.

Green Tip for Creating Less Water Pollution

If you replace household chemicals such as dishwashing liquid, laundry detergent, and toilet cleaner with more environmentally friendly products, you can reduce the amount of water pollution you create.

Other Ways You Can Use Less Water

✓ If you eat meat, try to limit the amount you consume.

✓ Try to use less paper. Paper production uses a huge amount of water. Recycle paper when you've finished with it.

✓ Ask your parents whether a rainwater tank can be installed. A tank makes use of the water that falls on your roof and means that you use less water from the main water supply.

Try eating less meat. Beef is not a very sustainable food choice, because it takes large amounts of water to produce.

Living Green Ratings and Green Tips

Pages 16–29 are filled with fun projects that will help you reduce the amount of water you use and protect Earth from pollution.

Each project is given its own Living Green star rating—from zero to five—as a measurement of how much the project lightens your environmental footprint.

Some projects give Green Tips telling you how you can improve the project's Living Green rating even more.

Green Tip

To improve the Living Green rating, make the strap from an old belt or a bicycle inner tube.

On each project spread, look for the Living Green rating. Five stars is the highest—and greenest—rating!

Living Green Rating
★ ★ ★ ★ ★

★ ★ ★	★ ★ ★ ★	★ ★ ★ ★ ★
A three-star project will teach you about an issue and explain how you are wasting natural resources or causing pollution.	A four-star project will show one or two ways to reduce garbage or pollution.	A five-star project will help you reduce garbage and pollution and actively protect the environment in many different ways.

How Much Water Do You Use?

Living Green Rating

★ ★ ★ ★

- Raises awareness of how much water your household uses
- Helps identify areas where you can reduce the amount of water you use

What You Need

- Pencil
- Calculator
- Photocopier

How a Home Uses Freshwater

Laundry 20%

Garden 20%

Kitchen 10%

Bathroom and toilet 50%

Complete a survey and compare your results with friends

If you want to save water, you first need to know how much water you use. Complete this survey to work out how much water your household uses each week.

What to Do

1. Ask your friends or classmates if they would like to complete a survey about their water use.

2. Photocopy the survey on pages 16–19. Give everyone a copy.

3. Complete the survey by studying your household's activities for one day. You may have to estimate the number of times you do some things each week, such as washing clothes. Use the calculator to help you answer the questions.

4. Compare your results with others.

5. In areas where you use a lot of water, can you think of ways to reduce your water use? See pages 20–29 for some ways to cut down your water usage.

About half of all the water used in a typical home is used in the bathroom and toilet. Find out how your home compares with this.

SURVEY

BATHROOM AND TOILET

A. How many showers are taken each day in your household? ....

B. How many gallons of water per minute does your shower use? ....
[Write down 4 if you have a standard shower head and 2.5 if you have a low-flow shower head.]

C. A x B x 7 (days) x 8 (minutes per shower) = ...

D. How many baths are taken each week in your household? ....

E. D x 25 (gallons per bath) = ...

F. How many times is the toilet flushed each day? ....

G. How many gallons of water does your toilet use per flush? ....
[Write down 3 if you have a standard toilet and 1 if you have a dual-flush toilet.]

H. F x G x 7 (days) = ...

I. How many times each day are taps used to shave, brush teeth, or wash hands and face? ....

J. How many minutes does the water run during each use?

....

K. I x J x 7 (days) x 1.5 (gallons per minute) =

....

SUBTOTAL:
Gallons of water used each week in the bathroom:
C + E + H + K =

....

SURVEY (CONTINUED)

KITCHEN

L. How many times are dishes washed by hand each day? ....

M. L x 7 (days) x 5 (gallons per wash) = ...

N. If you have a dishwasher, how many times is it used each week? ....

O. N x 10.5 (gallons per wash) = ...

P. How many gallons of water does your household use each day for cooking, cleaning, and drinking? ....
[Calculate 9 gallons per person.]

Q. P x 7 (days) = ...

SUBTOTAL: Gallons of water used each week in the kitchen:
M + O + Q = ...

LAUNDRY

R. How many loads of laundry are done each week? ....

S. How many gallons of water does your washing machine use for each load? ....
[Write down 21 if you have a front loader and 45 if you have a top loader.]

SUBTOTAL: Gallons of water used per week in the laundry:
R x S = ...

On average, front-loading washing machines use less than half the water of top loaders.

OUTDOORS

T. How many minutes per week do you run the garden hose? ....

U. T x 12 (gallons) = ...

V. How many watering cans of water do you fill with water each week? ....

W. V x 2.5 (gallons) = ...

SUBTOTAL: Gallons of water used outdoors each week: U + W = ...

TOTALS

X. To find the total number of gallons of water your household uses each week, add up the subtotals from each section = ...

Y. To find the average number of gallons of water your household uses each day: X ÷ 7 = ...

A lawn sprinkler wastes a lot of water. It is not a sustainable way of watering the garden.

How Much Water Do You Waste?

Living Green Rating

★ ★ ★

• Raises awareness of how much water you can waste through a dripping or running tap

What You Need

• Measuring pitcher, marked in fluid ounces
• Stopwatch or other timer
• Paper
• Pencil

If your tap drips, tell an adult and help save water and Earth!

Try these experiments to find out how much water you waste

Two common ways of wasting water are not fixing dripping taps and running the tap while you brush your teeth. Try these experiments to find out how much water you might be wasting like this.

How Much Water Does a Dripping Tap Waste?

What to Do

1. Turn on the tap and then adjust the flow of water so that it becomes just a drip.

2. Put the measuring pitcher underneath the tap.

3. Leave it for five minutes. Use the stopwatch to time yourself.

4. Write down the number of fluid ounces of water that have collected in the measuring pitcher.

5. Double this number.

6. Your answer is roughly the number of fluid ounces of water a dripping tap wastes in a week.

What You Need

- Large measuring pitcher, marked in fluid ounces
- Stopwatch or other timer
- Calculator
- Paper
- Pencil

How Much Water Do You Waste When You Brush Your Teeth?

What to Do

1. Turn on the bathroom tap.

2. Place the measuring pitcher underneath the tap.

3. Leave it for exactly five seconds. Use the stopwatch to time yourself.

4. Write down the number of fluid ounces of water in the pitcher.

5. Divide this number by three.

6. The answer is roughly the number of fluid ounces of water you waste each week if you leave the tap on while you brush your teeth.

Green Tip

To reduce the amount of water you waste at home:
- switch off the tap while you brush your teeth
- fix dripping taps as soon as you notice them
- switch off the water in the shower while you apply soap or shampoo
- instead of rinsing food scraps down the sink or into the waste disposal unit, scrape them into a trash can and add them to a compost heap

Make a Rain Gauge

Keep track of how much it has rained

One way of saving water is to water your plants only when they need it. By making a rain gauge you can keep track of the amount of rain your garden receives. This will help you avoid unnecessary watering.

Living Green Rating

★ ★ ★ ★

- Helps you save water by showing you rainfall levels so you know when not to water your plants
- Reduces **landfill**, because the plastic drink bottle is not thrown out as garbage

What You Need

- 0.5-gallon (2-liters) plastic drink bottle
- Scissors
- Paper clips
- Packet of gelatin crystals
- Mixing bowl
- Spoon
- Tea kettle
- Water
- Ruler
- Permanent marker
- Gravel or sand

Use an old plastic drink bottle, some gelatin and a few household items to make your own rain gauge.

Take care when cutting the top off the bottle and when boiling the water for the gelatin ⚠️

What to Do

1. Cut the top off the bottle about a quarter of the way down.

2. Prepare the gelatin according to the instructions on the packet. Usually this is by combining the gelatin crystals and boiling water in a mixing bowl.

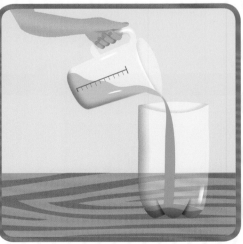

3. When the gelatin has cooled but is still liquid, pour some into the bottom part of the bottle. Pour up to where the bottle reaches its widest point.

4. Once the gelatin has set, use a ruler and marker to draw an inch scale on the side of the bottle. Start measuring from the top of the gelatin.

5. Take off the lid, and then place the top part of the bottle upside down in the bottom part of the bottle.

6. Secure with paper clips. This is your rain gauge!

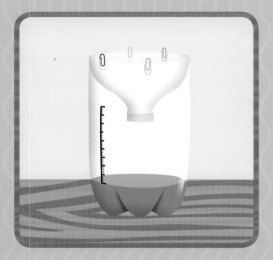

7. Place the rain gauge outside in an open space.

8. Place gravel or sand around the bottom of your rain gauge to help it stand upright.

9. Take rainfall readings from your rain gauge at the same time every day. To do this, remove the rain gauge from the sand or gravel. Place it on a flat surface and read the water level against the inch scale. Remember to empty the water out of the rain gauge before putting it back.

Green Tip

To improve the Living Green rating, empty the water from the rain gauge over an indoor plant that needs watering.

Make a Rain Catcher

Catch water that would normally be lost

A rain catcher can be used on areas such as a driveway, patio, or deck. The rain catcher will collect the water so you can save it instead of letting the water run off into the gutter. This will give you your own personal water supply!

Living Green Rating

★ ★ ★ ★

• Reduces the need to use water from the tap by collecting freshwater that would normally end up in the gutter and washed out to sea

What You Need

• Tarpaulin
• 4 buckets
• 4 bricks

What to Do

1. Choose an area of hard landscaping, such as a driveway, patio, or deck. To make sure your rain catcher collects as much water as possible, check that the area you have chosen is not sheltered by anything, such as a roof, patio umbrella, or overhanging trees.

2. Unfold the tarpaulin and place it flat on the ground.

3. Put an upside down bucket underneath each of the four corners of the tarpaulin.

4. Place a brick on top of each bucket to hold the tarpaulin in place.

Don't waste the rain that falls from the sky. Make your own rain catcher!

5. Wait for it to rain.

6. When the rain has stopped, empty your rain catcher carefully. To do this, remove the bricks from the buckets, and then turn one of the buckets the right way up. Lift up the other three corners of the tarpaulin and pour the water in the tarpaulin into the bucket you turned the right way up. You might need someone else to help you do this.

The water from your rain catcher is not safe to drink ⚠

7. Use the water around the house. This will help you reduce the amount of water you use from the tap!

Green Tip

Use your rain catcher water for:
- watering the garden or house plants
- washing the car
- cleaning the outside of the house
- flushing the toilet

Spectacular Solar Still

Turn saltwater into freshwater

Living Green Rating

★ ★ ★ ★ ★

• Reduces the need to use water from the tap because it creates freshwater from saltwater
• It could save your life!

What You Need

• Large bowl
• Cup
• Water
• Salt
• Teaspoon
• Plastic wrap
• Waterproof tape
• Scissors
• Small stone

In situations where clean drinking water is not available, knowing how to make a solar still could save your life! A solar still produces clean freshwater from any water source and from any type of water, even saltwater.

What to Do

1. Pour an inch (2.5 centimeters) of water into the bottom of the bowl.

2. Add a few teaspoons of salt and stir well. Taste the water. It is now saltwater and will taste salty.

3. Place the bowl outdoors in direct sunlight.

4. Place the cup in the center of the bowl. Take care not to splash any saltwater into the cup.

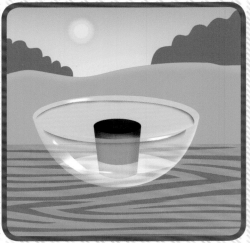

A few household items can help you transform saltwater into freshwater that is good enough to drink!

5. Place the plastic wrap over the bowl. Push it down in the center so that it comes to a point above the top of the cup. It should not touch the cup.

6. Place the small stone on top of the plastic wrap, directly above the cup.

7. Put waterproof tape all around the edge of the plastic wrap, where it touches the sides of the bowl. Make sure there are no gaps, so you can trap as much moisture as possible.

8. Leave your solar still in the sun for a few hours.

9. Wait for water to collect in the cup. Be patient, it may take several hours. When there is water in the cup, taste it. It should not taste salty at all!

Spray Cleaner and Greener

Make a **biodegradable** cleaner

Living Green Rating

★ ★ ★ ★

- Reduces the need to buy spray cleaner, so less environmental impact
- Uses natural ingredients, so no toxic chemicals are released to pollute the water system

Use this biodegradable spray cleaner to keep your bathroom and kitchen clean without contaminating the water supply with harmful chemicals. It costs a fraction of the price of store-bought cleaners.

What You Need

- Measuring cup
- Large bowl
- 1 cup water
- 1 cup white vinegar
- 2 tablespoons lemon juice or 1 lemon
- Teaspoon
- 5 teaspoons **baking soda**
- Wooden spoon
- Pitcher
- Funnel
- 20-fluid-ounce (600-milliliter) spray bottle
- Essential oil (optional)

You can make an Earth-friendly spray cleaner from just a few cheap ingredients.

What to Do

1. Pour the water and the white vinegar into a large bowl.

2. Add 2 tablespoons of lemon juice.

3. Add 1 teaspoon of baking soda. Wait for the fizzing to stop and then add another spoonful. Repeat until you have added 5 teaspoons of baking soda.

4. Use the wooden spoon to stir the mixture well.

5. If you are using an essential oil, add between six and eight drops. For a fresh smell, try lemongrass, lime, or mandarin essential oil. Stir again.

6. Pour the mixture into a pitcher.

7. Put a funnel into the top of the spray bottle. Pour the mixture into the bottle through the funnel.

8. Screw the spray top on the bottle.

9. Your spray cleaner can be used on most hard surfaces, including stoves, refrigerators, sinks, baths, showers, toilets, tiles, and kitchen counters. It is not suitable for use on wood, glass, or soft surfaces.

Green Tip

To make an environmentally friendly glass cleaner, make this spray cleaner but leave out the baking soda and the essential oils.

Find Out More About Living Green

The Internet is a great way of finding out more about how water use affects the environment and what you can do to use water more sustainably.

Useful Websites

Visit these useful websites:

http://unep.org/tunza/children
This website from the United Nations has downloadable fact sheets about environmental issues, tips for living more sustainably, and competitions you can enter.

www.water-pollution.org.uk
This website explains the complicated subject of water pollution in a way that makes it easy to understand. It also has links to other water pollution sites.

www.wateruseitwisely.com
This website has more than one hundred tips for saving water. It also has a fun kids section.

Searching for Information

Here are some terms you might enter into your Internet search bar to find out more about water use and the environment:

- water pollution
- recycled water
- water shortage
- irrigation and desertification

Glossary

baking soda White, powdery chemical compound used for cooking and cleaning; also called sodium bicarbonate or bicarb soda.

biodegradable Able to rot away or be broken down naturally without harming the environment.

condenses Changes form from a gas into a liquid, such as when water vapor changes into water.

contaminated Having harmful substances in it, such as waste or chemicals.

detergents Liquid or powder cleaning materials that clean away dirt and oil.

disinfectants Substances, usually liquids, that are used to kill bacteria.

environment The natural world, including plants, animals, land, rivers, and oceans.

evaporates Changes form from a liquid into a gas, such as when water changes into water vapor.

fertilizers Substances added to the soil to help crops grow.

fossil fuels Coal, oil, and natural gas, which are natural resources that are formed from the remains of dead plants and animals, deep under Earth's surface, over millons of years.

global warming The process by which Earth's average temperature is getting warmer.

habitat Place where plants and animals live.

irrigation Supplying water to a dry area to help crops grow.

landfill Garbage that is buried and covered with soil at garbage dumps.

manufactured Made from raw materials into a product for people to buy and use.

natural resources Natural materials that can be used by people, such as wood, metal, coal, and water.

nonrenewable resources Natural resources that cannot be easily replaced, such as coal, oil. and natural gas.

pesticides Poisonous chemicals used to kill pests, such as insects, fungi, and weeds, to prevent them from damaging crops.

pollution Damaging substances, especially chemicals or waste products, that harm the environment.

precipitation Any form of water that falls from the sky, such as rain, snow, sleet, or hail.

renewable resources Natural resources that will never run out, such as the wind, or that can easily be replaced, such as wood.

toxic Poisonous to living things.

water vapor Water in the form of gas.

Index